The Human Factor

David Lask

Published by David Lask, 2024.

While every precaution has been taken in the preparation of this book, the publisher assumes no responsibility for errors or omissions, or for damages resulting from the use of the information contained herein.

THE HUMAN FACTOR

First edition. March 1, 2024.

ISBN: 979-8224828777

Written by David Lask.

Table of Contents

Introduction

In today's fast-paced, ever-evolving world, success often hinges on the ability to communicate, negotiate, and build connections. But what if success isn't about outsmarting or overpowering others? What if there's a secret to achieving your goals that also empowers those around you? Welcome to "The Human Factor: Mastering the Art of Win-Win Communication."

Let's provide you with a glimpse of the promise, intrigue, and identification of the need that weaves through the fabric of this book. It's our assurance that this journey will transform your approach to life, relationships, and negotiation.

From these pages, you will emerge equipped with the tools and insights needed to transform your life. We promise that by the end of this journey, you'll understand that there's more to communication and negotiation than meets the eye. It's a journey of self-discovery that will unlock the art of reaching mutual success. Whether you're seeking growth in your personal relationships or looking to make waves in the business world, "The Human Factor" is your indispensable roadmap.

Picture this: a world where every interaction is a triumph, where you never feel isolated in your pursuits. Imagine a life where every relationship is a source of mutual growth, and every negotiation concludes with both sides walking away satisfied. It's a reality that might seem like a dream, but it's one that this book will help you craft.

Intrigue pulses through the heart of "The Human Factor." In the upcoming chapters, you'll explore tales of everyday people achieving remarkable outcomes by embracing the power of win-win communication. These stories unveil the transformative potential in your own life, showing you that a different way of engaging with the world is not only possible but within your grasp.

We live in an age teeming with conflicting interests, adversarial approaches, and divisive rhetoric. There's an urgent need for a new way of communicating, one that fosters understanding and unity. "The Human Factor" answers that need. It is your comprehensive guide to effective communication, empathetic negotiation, and building stronger connections. Whether you're seeking personal growth, improved relationships, or greater professional success, our book has the solution you've been searching for.

The principles shared within these pages are not mere theoretical musings. They're distilled from the real-life experiences of countless individuals who have harnessed the human factor to redefine their lives. The stories in this book transcend cultural, geographical, and professional boundaries, showing that this path is open to anyone willing to take it.

"The Human Factor" isn't just a book; it's an immersive journey. As we explore the concept, you'll explore the intricacies of win-win communication and negotiation, delving into the nuances of the human factor's impact on every aspect of your life. It's an adventure through the human experience, and it starts right here.

Are you prepared to embark on this transformative voyage? Let's take the first step together and dive into "The Human Factor."

Chapter 1 — UNDERSTANDING THE HUMAN FACTOR

"The most important thing in communication is hearing what isn't said."
Peter Drucker

Welcome to the exciting journey of understanding and mastering the human factor. I'll share personal experiences that have profoundly influenced my perspective on effective communication and negotiation. It's through these experiences that I've come to grasp the true power of the human factor. The human factor is not just another buzzword; it's a powerful concept that can transform the way we interact with others. We'll define the human factor and explain its significance in a variety of situations, from personal relationships to professional dealings.

To make the concept more tangible, we'll share real-life examples of situations where the human factor played a pivotal role. These anecdotes will illustrate the difference between win-lose and win-win approaches to communication. Communication isn't just about words; it's also about emotions and psychology. We'll delve into the underlying psychological and emotional aspects of the human factor, shedding light on why it works so effectively.

Back in high school, I often felt like a nerd, but I had a unique knack for connecting with people. I befriended those who were often picked on, and my ability to befriend even the toughest individuals was a mystery to me at the time. What I didn't realize then was that I was effectively communicating with them in a way that made them feel heard, understood, and liked. They knew I didn't judge them, and I provided honest feedback without being rude or condescending. Skills from the foundation for understanding the human factor.

As I progressed to college, I began to realize that effective communication went beyond personal relationships—it had the potential to shape my professional future. I discovered that by skillfully engaging with people, I could not only advance my own goals but also help others achieve what they desired. It was a win-win approach to communication, and it was a powerful tool for success.

In the journey to understanding the human factor, I've encountered numerous challenges where traditional win-lose approaches simply didn't yield the right outcomes. For instance, there was a time when

I couldn't convince a Chief Information Officer (CIO) to adopt my email system proposal. Instead of pushing my idea aggressively, I took a different route. I lightened the atmosphere and playfully pointed out the potential drawbacks of not choosing my proposal.

After about six months with the CIO's email system, it was shown through the limitations of the current email system that my proposal was more feature rich while remaining more secure. We then proceeded to migrate to the email system that we, as a group, had agreed was a better proposal. That email system is still in use to this day. Sometimes, you need to gracefully accept a "loss" to demonstrate the value of your idea.

The primary obstacle to achieving a win-win mindset in communication and negotiation, I've found, is ego. It's challenging for individuals to step outside their own perspectives and acknowledge the validity of someone else's viewpoint. Admitting that one's idea could be wrong can be difficult, but it's a crucial step in adopting the human factor approach.

In the tapestry of human interactions, empathy emerges quietly as a powerful thread, weaving connections and fostering understanding. Its significance often goes unnoticed, yet it stands as a vital cornerstone of the human factor. Let me illustrate this with a poignant experience that transcends specific circumstances, demonstrating the universal relevance of empathy.

In a challenging chapter of life, I found myself in the role of a mediator, guiding individuals through the stormy seas of a difficult divorce. The emotions were raw, grievances were plentiful, and the air was thick with tension. However, amid the turmoil, empathy emerged as a guiding light. Instead of succumbing to the weight of personal animosities, I chose to anchor the process in empathy, a force capable of bridging the gaps between conflicting perspectives.

The focal point became the needs of the most vulnerable party involved—the child. By channeling empathy, I steered both parties away from the perilous shores of self-righteousness, helping them to recognize the shared responsibility of safeguarding their child's well-being. In this narrative, the specifics of the divorce become secondary; what takes precedence is the universal truth that empathy, when harnessed with intention, has the power to transform conflict into collaboration.

This tale is not confined to the realm of divorces; it echoes through various life scenarios where human relationships are tested. It serves as a reminder that empathy, often underestimated in its potency, can untangle the knots of discord, and illuminate the path toward shared understanding. In the intricate dance of human connection, empathy takes center stage, inviting us all to recognize the shared humanity that binds us, transcending the boundaries of individual experiences.

I've often found myself in situations where active listening proved indispensable. For instance, when my boss expressed frustration over a stalled project, I could have taken the path of reluctance, fearing that my boss would claim all the credit. However, I realized that by actively listening, collaborating with colleagues, and contributing innovative ideas, I could not only ignite the project but also position myself as a proactive team player. This approach benefited both my career and the organization.

Think about this and imagine a family at a crossroads, facing a pivotal decision about whether to relocate to a different city in pursuit of a better job opportunity. In this moment, the human factor emerges as a guiding light, influencing their choices. As they deliberate, they not only consider the practical aspects of the move but also the emotional well-being of their children. They recognize the potential strains this decision may place on their marriage and acknowledge the importance of maintaining connections with their extended family. Here, empathy and understanding come into play as they navigate a complex web of considerations, prioritizing not just personal gain but the collective happiness and harmony of their family unit.

Now, let's shift our focus to the dynamics of friendships. Picture a scenario where a tight-knit group of friends excitedly plans a vacation together. Each member of the group brings their unique preferences and desires for the trip, setting the stage for potential disagreements. However, understanding the human factor within their friendships guides them toward compromise and collaboration. Instead of stubbornly pursuing individual desires, they empathize with one another, finding common ground, and making decisions that ensure everyone's satisfaction. The human factor in their friendships transforms potential conflicts into opportunities for growth and strengthened bonds.

In the corporate world, consider a crisis within a company, one that breeds anxiety and uncertainty among its employees. Here, the human factor takes center stage as company leadership responds with empathy and foresight. Rather than making decisions in isolation, they engage with their workforce, addressing concerns, providing much-needed support, and involving employees in the decision-making process. This approach not only helps alleviate anxiety but also fosters trust and a sense of unity during challenging times. It's a testament to the power of the human factor in corporate leadership, where compassion and understanding lead to resilience and shared success.

In this chapter, we've explored the foundations of the human factor and how it has shaped my perspective on communication and negotiation. I hope you, as a reader, are beginning to reflect on moments in your life where the human factor could have made a difference—a difference that might not have been immediate but could have set the stage for a more beneficial future.

In the upcoming chapters, we will delve deeper into the principles of the human factor and provide practical strategies for incorporating them into your life. So, get ready to explore this transformative approach to communication and negotiation further.

EXCERCISES

WIN-WIN CHALLENGE

Reach out to someone from a different cultural background and engage in a conversation. Try to understand their perspective on a topic you both care about.

WIN-WIN INSIGHTS

"Embracing the human factor means recognizing that beneath our differences, we share common values and emotions. When we tap into this shared humanity, we can build bridges."

Chapter 2 — BREAKING FREE FROM THE WIN-LOSE MINDSET

"The real voyage of discovery consists not in seeking new landscapes, but in having new eyes."
    ~ Marcel Proust

In the realm of effective communication and negotiation, it's crucial to recognize the limitations of the win-lose mindset—the "my way or the highway" approach. Throughout my journey, I've encountered individuals who embraced this mindset, and while some situations saw moments of success, the overall outcomes were often marred by failure.

One such instance stands out—a company with a CEO who firmly believed in his absolute authority. This CEO's unwavering attitude created a culture of fear within the organization, resulting in a revolving door of senior executive staff. The company stagnated and, in some ways, regressed. However, a unit of the company took matters into their own hands, breaking free from the old owner's grasp and starting a new company. Today, that new venture thrives, and during my time as a consultant, I even had the privilege of assisting them on several projects. It was a testament to the power of shedding the win-lose mindset and embracing collaboration.

To break free from the win-lose mindset, one must understand that it's not about manipulation or doing whatever it takes to get one's way. It's about choosing the right battles to win and gracefully losing to the others. The motivation to transition from a win-lose to a win-win mindset can come from various sources, but for me, it was the birth of my daughter. I wanted to provide her with everything she could want and instill in her a desire to help others. My grandmother's wisdom echoed in my mind: "It's not about winning all the battles to win the war. Winning the right battles and accepting losses gracefully is the key to ultimate success."

In dealing with individuals entrenched in a win-lose mindset, you may encounter resistance. Some people firmly believe they are always right and that you are wrong. This can hinder effective communication and negotiation if not handled carefully. The strategy here is to identify even a single point of agreement and nurture it, making the other person feel it was their idea. This approach plants a seed of change in them, gradually shifting their mindset toward collaboration.

There will be times when nothing you say or do can guarantee a collaborative result. In such situations, it's crucial to lose gracefully and live to fight another day. Again, my grandmother's words echo in my mind, reminding me that I am always in a state of growth, not always in a battle. I once sought to become the manager of my department, and despite my skills and connections, I wasn't given the opportunity. It was a case of being a victim of my own success; I was excellent at solving problems, and they knew it. But instead of becoming disheartened, I used this as a catalyst for personal growth. I honed my communication and networking skills, becoming the go-to person for colleagues facing challenges. While it wasn't the traditional win, it was a substantial form of growth.

Now, you might be wondering how to transition from the win-lose mindset to the more collaborative win-win approach. I won't sugarcoat it; it's not easy, and it's not for everyone. However, with the will and desire to change, anyone can do it. Start by eliminating "no" from your conversations. Replace it with a more open-minded approach, such as "let's see what we can do." People are more willing to listen and cooperate when they sense your willingness to help and your openness to finding mutual solutions.

Let's delve into various scenarios where the win-lose mindset often takes center stage. Picture a family scene where two siblings are locked in constant competition, vying for their parents' attention and approval. In this battle for recognition, it may seem that one's success diminishes others. However, breaking free from the win-lose mindset means helping these siblings recognize that their individual achievements can coexist harmoniously, enriching the family rather than causing conflict.

Now, let's shift our focus to the corporate world, where employees often find themselves in fierce competition for promotions and recognition. The win-lose mindset can lead to a cutthroat environment, hindering collaboration and knowledge sharing. However, breaking free from this mentality involves fostering a workplace culture that encourages employees to collaborate, share their expertise, and collectively work towards the success of the entire team.

Lastly, consider the realm of politics, where opposing parties frequently engage in heated debates without seeking common ground. The win-lose mindset in politics can hinder progress and compromise. But breaking free from this mindset involves finding areas of agreement, encouraging cooperation on shared objectives, and ultimately serving the best interests of the constituents.

We will now delve deeper into the practical strategies and techniques required to fully embrace the win-win mindset. It's a journey that demands effort, patience, and a commitment to personal and professional growth.

So, take that first step by removing "no" from your vocabulary and embracing the possibilities that lie ahead.

EXERCISES

WIN-WIN CHALLENGE

Identify a recent conflict in your life and reflect on how your ego may have played a role in it. Next time, try to approach a similar situation with a win-win mindset.

WIN-WIN INSIGHTS

"Letting go of the need to 'win' in every situation can be liberating. A win-win mindset opens doors to creative solutions and stronger relationships."

Chapter 3 — THE POWER OF EMPATHY

"When you show deep empathy toward others, their defensive energy goes down, and positive energy replaces it. That's when you can get more creative in solving problems."
~ Stephen Covey

In our journey to understand the human factor, we arrive at a critical crossroads—empathy. This deceptively simple yet immensely powerful ability allows us to not just understand but truly share the feelings of others. It's about walking in someone else's shoes, seeing life through their eyes, and genuinely caring about their experiences.

So, what exactly is empathy? It's the capacity to understand or feel what another person is experiencing from within their frame of reference. It's the ability to emotionally understand what other people feel, to see things from their point of view, and to imagine ourselves in their place.

Empathy is not a foreign concept to me; it's something I've practiced since my early days. Back in grade school, I witnessed kids being picked on and made fun of. Instead of joining in, I took a different approach. I imagined how it would feel to be in their position, isolated and ridiculed. This early experience planted the seeds of empathy within me, setting the stage for a lifelong journey of understanding and connecting with others.

But why is empathy so important, you might ask? The answer lies in the profound impact it has on both the giver and the receiver. It's not just about making others feel heard and valued; it's about forging deeper connections and fostering positivity.

Empathy isn't a static skill; it evolves over time. It's not merely a tool for dealing with difficult people; it's a fundamental aspect of effective communication and negotiation. When you genuinely care about seeing things from another person's perspective, a remarkable transformation occurs in your interactions.

Consider this: in negotiations or any situation where others believe you're not truly there to listen, empathy becomes your secret weapon. People begin to realize that you're not just interested in getting your way; you're genuinely concerned about their viewpoint. When they feel heard and understood, walls break down, and a sense of collaboration emerges.

Now, let's explore scenarios that vividly illustrate the power of empathy in various aspects of life. Imagine a compassionate teacher who notices a student struggling academically. The teacher's empathy shines when they take the time to genuinely understand the student's challenges, offering unwavering support and adapting teaching methods to cater to the student's unique needs. This empathetic approach leads to a transformation, with the struggling student experiencing significant academic improvement.

In a healthcare setting, we encounter a nurse caring for a terminally ill patient. Here, the power of empathy becomes palpable as the nurse extends beyond medical care, providing profound emotional support to the patient. In the patient's final days, this empathy brings comfort and peace, not only to the patient but possibly the patient's family, elevating the quality of their experience during a challenging time.

Now, shift your focus to a family dealing with a significant conflict. Here, empathy emerges as the cornerstone of resolution. Family members actively listen to one another's perspectives, genuinely acknowledge each other's feelings, and work collaboratively to find solutions that prioritize the well-being of everyone involved. This powerful display of empathy not only resolves conflicts but also strengthens the bonds within the family.

So, how can you develop your empathy skills? It's not a switch you can flip overnight, but with time, practice, and determination, you can expand your capacity for empathy. Start with the basics; think about your pets. Visualize their emotions, their moments of joy, sadness, and peace. Imagine the contentment of your dog basking in the sun, smelling the air, and feeling the peacefulness in their hearts. It's about experiencing the world through their senses, and in doing so, you begin to feel the joy that others experience.

Empathy is a powerful tool in everyday communication. A simple "thank you" and "have a good day" to a grocery store clerk or a bank teller can brighten their day. It's like passing on a spark of joy, creating a ripple effect of positivity.

But what about challenging situations? Can empathy bridge the gap with individuals who hold opposing views or interests? The answer is yes. Take, for instance, a time when I told the CFO that a project couldn't be completed within the timeframe he desired. His initial reaction was one of shock. However, by repositioning my response with empathy, the situation shifted dramatically. Instead of escalating the issue, I acknowledged the resources at our disposal, fostering an environment where success became achievable.

Empathy is a transformative force that leads to understanding, connection, and ultimately, win-win solutions. As we continue our exploration of the human factor, remember that empathy isn't just a skill to acquire; it's a mindset to embrace. It's about genuinely caring, seeking to understand, and making the world a better place one empathetic interaction at a time.

EXERCISES

WIN-WIN CHALLENGE

Choose an issue you're passionate about and discuss it with someone who holds an opposing view. Practice active listening and empathy during the conversation.

WIN-WIN INSIGHTS

"Empathy is the bridge to understanding. It's about walking in someone else's shoes without judgment. This connection can lead to common ground."

Chapter 4 — ACTIVE LISTENING - THE KEY TO UNDERSTANDING

"The most important thing in communication is to hear what isn't being said."

~ Peter Drucker

Active listening, a transformative skill, transcends both personal and professional life. It's the ability to not just hear but truly understand and respond effectively, a skill that can make all the difference in resolving conflicts, fostering cooperation, and achieving mutual success.

In both personal and professional contexts, active listening plays a pivotal role. At home, you might occasionally receive feedback from family members about your listening skills. This feedback holds some truth, yet it's essential to realize that in professional environments, active listening is a continuous demand. In these settings, your mind remains alert, your ears attuned, and your brain engaged.

Let's explore the power of active listening through a real-life professional scenario. Picture a project meeting where two units, IT and Business, were locked in a tense standoff. The IT team was focused on network security, while the Business unit was adamant about acquiring remote access through VPN.

At first glance, it appeared to be a classic case of conflicting interests. But active listening came to the rescue. By tuning in to what each side truly wanted and what they were unwilling to compromise on {what} , I was able to insert myself into the conversation. I offered an alternative that would satisfy both parties: only select technical personnel in the Business unit would have Virtual Private Network (VPN) access, while others could use remote desktop services.

Through active listening and timely intervention, a win-win solution emerged. The IT team-maintained network security, and the Business unit gained the access they needed. The key takeaway here is that active listening can bridge gaps, transform standoffs into collaborative discussions, and lead to mutually beneficial resolutions.

Picture a marriage where miscommunication and misunderstandings often overshadow moments of connection. In this intimate setting, active listening and effective communication become the guiding lights for the couple's journey. Instead of talking past each other, they discover the art of listening attentively, seeking clarity through thoughtful questions, and expressing their thoughts with precision. As a result, their interactions transform into healthier, more harmonious exchanges, strengthening the bonds that drew them together in the first place.

Now, shift the scene to the realm of customer service. Imagine a frustrated customer grappling with a complex issue. Here, the spotlight shines on active listening and effective communication. A dedicated customer service representative steps in, poised to unravel the intricacies of the customer's problem. With patience and genuine attentiveness, the representative listens intently, delving deeper into insightful questions. They remain unwavering in their commitment to ensuring the customer's issue is not just resolved but resolved to their utmost satisfaction.

In the bustling landscape of the workplace, conflicts may arise due to miscommunication among team members. It's a scenario we've all encountered. In this context, active listening and effective communication become the linchpin of resolution. Team members embrace open discussions, actively paraphrasing one another's statements to ensure understanding, and collaboratively work through differences in a constructive manner. These skills not only mend frayed relations but also fortify the team's ability to achieve collective goals.

Active listening is a skill that improves over time. As you immerse yourself in the world of active listening, you may find that your brain seemingly remains in an "always on" mode. It's true; active listening requires constant alertness, as you never know when you'll need that nugget of information.

However, it's vital to balance this state with periods of decompression. Your mind needs breaks from active listening, just as your body needs rest. Engage in activities like reading, watching TV, playing video games, or gardening to allow your mind to "float" and recharge. These breaks are essential to maintain your active listening skills effectively.

Improving your active listening skills is an ongoing journey. You might already be practicing it, perhaps without even realizing. Consider those moments when you're out in public, glancing at a menu in a restaurant or perusing store shelves. You overhear someone exclaim, "Oh, wow!" Naturally, your curiosity is piqued, and you turn to see what's caught their attention.

This, too, is active listening in action. When you respond by suggesting a similar item or sharing your enthusiasm, you're not merely hearing; you're actively engaging with your surroundings. It's about staying attuned to the world around you and seizing opportunities to contribute positively.

As previously stated, I think it is worth restating that "active listening isn't just about hearing; it's about understanding and responding effectively". It plays a significant role in shaping win-win solutions. In the example mentioned earlier, active listening allowed me to identify the core concerns of both the IT and Business units. By addressing these concerns creatively, I facilitated a mutually beneficial outcome.

In your own professional experiences, you'll likely encounter situations where active listening serves as the linchpin for collaboration and resolution. It's a skill that helps parties find common ground, navigate conflicts, and achieve shared success.

As we continue our exploration of the human factor, remember that active listening is a dynamic skill that evolves with practice and self-awareness. It's a tool that empowers you to connect with others, transform conflicts into opportunities, and lead conversations toward win-win solutions.

EXERCISES

WIN-WIN CHALLENGE

The next time you find yourself in a heated argument, try to actively listen to the other person without interruption. Reflect on how the dynamics of the conversation change.

WIN-WIN INSIGHTS

"Active listening isn't just about hearing words; it's about understanding the emotions behind them. It can turn a confrontation into a constructive dialogue."

Chapter 5 — EGO AND ITS ROLE IN COMMUNICATION

"Out beyond ideas of wrongdoing and right doing, there is a field. I'll meet you there."

~ Rumi

Ego, that intricate construct within each of us, often becomes a silent hindrance to effective communication and negotiation. It's essential to recognize that ego is not an inherently negative trait; rather, it's a mindset that surfaces in varying degrees in every individual at different points in life. Understanding this concept is the first step toward mastering the art of communication.

In my journey, I've encountered individuals with the most formidable egos. One memorable experience involved working closely with someone whose ego seemed larger than life itself. Our conversations were often challenging, and more often than not, communication seemed to break down. However, amidst these apparent failures, I discovered something crucial—a silver lining in each interaction.

The key takeaway from these experiences was that even within the most ego-driven conversations, there was always something valuable to extract. It might take time, persistence, and the application of skills like active listening and empathy, but I learned to uncover common ground. Over time, this common ground could serve as the foundation for a win-win situation.

Ego, in the context of communication and negotiation, can manifest in various ways. It's essential to discern the signs and markers of ego-driven communication. Think of it as engaging in a conversation with a constitutional lawyer—everything is presented as fact, and their interpretation of the law is often portrayed as the only way. Recognize that they are not necessarily wrong; they are merely entrenched in their perspective. In such situations, it's vital to identify areas where compromise is possible and gently steer the conversation toward mutual understanding.

To manage or defuse ego-driven conversations, focus on finding the common objectives, however small they may be. Even the tiniest shared interest can be the bridge to defusing tension and building trust. The goal is to create an environment where the other party feels that the outcome aligns with their interests or, better yet, that they have played a significant role in shaping it. This is not manipulation; it's a strategic approach to reach a win-win solution.

Developing self-awareness to recognize your own ego in communication is a vital step toward effective interaction. A practice that has proven helpful is to engage in self-reflection during and after conversations. Listen to yourself as if you were an outsider observing the interaction. Pay attention to how your words and tone may have come across and consider how you would feel if someone spoke to you in a similar manner.

Active listening to your own communication is an essential tool. Always remember that you are in an "always on" state, with your mind ready to actively engage in dialogue. Confidence and ego are not one and the same; confidence can coexist with humility, while ego tends to assert itself forcefully. Humility is a powerful ally in navigating ego-driven situations.

Picture the grand stage of international diplomacy, where two nations find themselves locked in a battle of opposing viewpoints over a critical issue. Here, the quest for common ground takes center stage as diplomats engage in intricate negotiations. Their goal is crystal clear: to unearth those precious patches of agreement and areas for compromise. Why? Because it's these very junctures that hold the promise of maintaining peace and stability on the global canvas.

Shifting gears to a more intimate setting, let's delve into the intricate world of parent-teen relationships. It's a realm notorious for conflicts, a testing ground where generational gaps often spark clashes. Yet, in this familial microcosm, the concept of finding common ground shines with exceptional importance. Here, parents and teenagers embark on a collaborative journey, one that involves setting rules and boundaries. These rules, when forged together, become more than just lines on paper; they are the threads that weave understanding and trust between generations.

Now, turn your gaze toward the vibrant realm of business. Picture two companies on the brink of a potential partnership, each with its unique strengths, aspirations, and vision for the future. Finding common ground in this context isn't just a notion but a strategic necessity. It involves the intricate process of identifying shared objectives, aligning corporate values, and skillfully negotiating terms that not only meet but exceed the needs of both parties. The outcome? A flourishing alliance, marked by success and mutual benefit, propelling both companies to new horizons of achievement.

In summary, ego is a complex facet of human interaction, present in varying degrees within us all. Learning to recognize, understand, and navigate ego in communication and negotiation is a journey that requires patience, self-awareness, and the application of skills like active listening, empathy, and humility. By doing so, you can transform ego-driven conversations into opportunities for mutual success and foster a win-win mindset.

EXERCISES

WIN-WIN CHALLENGE

Choose a situation where you have a vested interest. Identify three points of common ground between you and the other party and build your negotiation around these shared interests.

WIN-WIN INSIGHTS

"Common ground is the fertile soil where mutually beneficial solutions can grow. It's the foundation of successful win-win negotiations."

Chapter 6 — OVERCOMING OBSTACLES AND RESISTANCE

"The only way to do great work is to love what you do."
~ Steve Jobs

As we continue our exploration of win-win communication and negotiation, it's crucial to recognize that challenges and resistance are an intrinsic part of this journey. These obstacles often make their presence felt, whether we're navigating the intricate landscape of personal relationships or traversing the complex terrain of professional environments. To overcome these challenges, we must cultivate patience, resilience, and strategic thinking.

Let's begin with personal relationships, where differences of opinion are a common occurrence. Take, for example, a situation in my own life where effective win-win communication was put to the test - my relationship with my spouse. As many can sympathize or relate to, disagreements with a lawyer spouse can often feel like an uphill battle. However, the true essence of win-win communication doesn't solely revolve around winning arguments but rather hinges on the art of comprehending each other's viewpoints.

Through active listening and empathy, my spouse and I have learned to find common ground and acknowledge each other's feelings and perspectives, even when confronted with inevitable disagreements. This practice has not only fostered mutual understanding but has also strengthened our relationship over time.

Shifting our focus to the professional realm, obstacles can manifest in various forms. They may be rooted in rigid policies, unwavering procedures, or entrenched mindsets that resist change. Initially, these obstacles may appear insurmountable, but with the right approach, they can be transformed into opportunities for win-win outcomes.

In my professional journey, I encountered a situation where we urgently needed a larger server room with improved cooling. Initially, the CEO was resolute in his "no" due to concerns about costs and doubts regarding necessity. However, a transformative process unfolded over the course of two years {what happened}. A significant factor in this transformation was my commitment to not only displaying confidence in my abilities but also embracing a willingness to listen and accommodate the perspectives and needs of others. This flexibility and openness ultimately led to the construction of an upgraded server room, aligning our department's requirements with the broader organizational goals.

Maintaining motivation and focus on achieving win-win outcomes can be a formidable task, particularly when negotiations are prolonged, or obstacles persist. During such moments, it's crucial to keep the ultimate objective in mind.

Consider the analogy of parenthood, a journey that extends not just for months but for years, even decades. As parents, the primary aspiration is to witness our children thrive and lead fulfilling lives. Yet, this transformative journey unfolds gradually, demanding ongoing compromise and the ability to make tough decisions. Parenthood embodies an enduring win-win dynamic, where both parents and children work together toward mutual growth and happiness.

Let's shed some light on the multi-faceted nature of overcoming obstacles and resistance. It's a journey that spans from conserving nature's wonders to managing project teams and revolutionizing education—an art form that harmonizes diverse perspectives, embraces empathy, and champions the human factor in all its glory. Now, let's delve into the realm of overcoming obstacles and resistance, where the human factor often encounters its most formidable adversaries.

Picture, if you will, an environmental organization fueled by a mission to preserve nature's splendor, facing a daunting challenge. This challenge takes the shape of a community reluctant to lend their support to the noble cause of conservation. Here, the art of overcoming obstacles and resistance transforms into a delicate dance of engagement. The organization must listen attentively to the concerns of community members, earnestly address their reservations, and vividly illustrate how conservation initiatives hold the potential to elevate everyone's quality of life.

Shifting gears into the dynamic arena of project management, envision a project team moving full steam ahead. However, they encounter an unexpected roadblock—an internal one. Some team members dig their heels in resisting, a classic response to change. Overcoming these hurdles requires more than sheer determination; it demands the finesse of a skilled leader. A leader who not only listens to the concerns of team members but also acknowledges their unique perspectives. Together, they embark on a journey of collaborative problem-solving, striving to uncover solutions that not only advance the project but also cater to the individual needs and fears of the team members.

Think about the ever-evolving landscape of education, with a school district at the forefront, daring to implement innovative teaching methods. Here, the concept of overcoming obstacles and resistance takes center stage, for change often meets resistance in the hallowed halls of academia. The district's challenge lies in engaging with teachers, parents, and students alike, empathetically understanding their reservations and demonstrating, with unwavering conviction, how these innovations can transcend traditional boundaries. The goal? To enrich the educational experience for all stakeholders, paving the way for a brighter, more adaptive future.

Through my experiences, I've noticed recurring patterns in how people grapple with communication and negotiation processes. One prevalent pattern revolves around the belief that one's perspective is unequivocally correct, and any contrary viewpoint is categorically wrong. This resistance often finds its roots in external influences, deeply entrenched viewpoints, or a reluctance to consider alternative perspectives.

The win-win mindset centers on acknowledging everyone's right to their opinions and beliefs while fostering collaboration toward a common objective. Over time, individuals engaging in open and empathetic dialogue begin to recognize that the success of the team or department holds greater significance than any individual viewpoint or resistance.

In essence, this serves as a poignant reminder that obstacles and resistance are not adversaries but rather integral facets of the win-win communication and the negotiation journey. By acknowledging these challenges and addressing them with patience and empathy, we transform them into steppingstones toward mutually beneficial outcomes, whether in our personal lives or professional pursuits.

EXERCISES

WIN-WIN CHALLENGE

Think about a persistent obstacle you've faced. Write down three alternative approaches that incorporate a win-win mindset.

WIN-WIN INSIGHTS

"Resistance is an opportunity for creative problem-solving. When you embrace it, you'll find that even the most challenging obstacles can be transformed."

Chapter 7 — NEGOTIATING IN PERSONAL RELATIONSHIPS

"In every conceivable manner, the family is linked to our past, bridge to our future."
~ Alex Haley

When we think of win-win communication, it's often in the context of business negotiations or problem-solving at work. But its transformative power extends far beyond the professional realm. It can mend the rifts in our personal lives, creating bonds that thrive on mutual respect and understanding.

Imagine being in a marriage with someone whose profession is built on debate, like my spouse, a lawyer. It might seem like an unwinnable situation where every disagreement turns into a courtroom battle. However, we've learned that winning isn't the ultimate goal in personal relationships. Instead, it's about comprehending each other's perspectives, even when they diverge. Our disagreements have evolved into opportunities for deepening our understanding of one another through active listening and empathy.

In the realm of personal relationships, active listening plays a pivotal role. It's about being fully present when your loved one speaks, not just hearing their words but absorbing their emotions and intentions. When you truly listen, you create a safe space for them to express themselves, fostering a sense of trust and connection. When we try and use active listening it has been our anchor in moments of disagreement, allowing us to uncover the underlying emotions and concerns that might have gone unnoticed otherwise.

Empathy is another cornerstone of effective communication in personal relationships. It's the ability to step into the shoes of your loved ones, to understand their feelings and viewpoints. Empathy allows us to bridge gaps that differences in opinion might create. It's about acknowledging the emotions of the other person, even if you don't necessarily agree with their perspective.

My spouse and I have found that empathy is a powerful tool for navigating our personal disagreements. Instead of seeing each other as adversaries, we strive to understand each other's emotional landscapes. When my spouse, passionately argues a point, I try to place myself in her shoes. I imagine the weight of their responsibilities and the pressures she faces in her profession. This doesn't mean I always concede, but it means I approach our discussions with compassion and a genuine desire to understand.

In personal relationships, conflicts are not signs of failure but opportunities for growth. They allow us to learn more about our loved ones and ourselves. When we engage in human factor style communication, we shift the focus from winning an argument to strengthening the relationship. It's about finding common ground, compromising when needed, and, above all, ensuring that both parties feel heard and valued.

Take, for instance, a situation where you and your partner disagree on a major life decision, such as where to live or how to raise your children. These are not minor issues, and differing opinions can lead to tension. However, by applying these new principles, you can transform these conflicts into discussions that ultimately strengthen your bond.

In our marriage, we've faced such decisions, and they were not always easy. But by actively listening to each other's dreams, concerns, and fears, we were able to find compromises that allowed us to move forward together. The win-win mindset isn't about one person winning and the other losing: it's about both parties winning through understanding, empathy, and compromise.

In addition to conflict resolution, human factor communication can be instrumental in deepening your connections with loved ones. It's about creating an atmosphere where each person feels valued, understood, and supported. When you practice active listening and empathy consistently, you send a powerful message: "I care about you, and your feelings matter to me."

Think about the times when you've felt truly heard and understood by someone close to you. It's a transformative experience that strengthens the bond between you.

It's about more than just reaching agreements; it's about nurturing understanding, empathy, and resilience in the sacred spaces where human connections thrive. So, let's delves more into the intricate world of negotiating in personal relationships, where the human factor takes center stage, showcasing its adaptability and resilience.

Picture a marriage counseling scenario—an intimate space where a couple grapples with the challenges that life has thrown their way. In this deeply personal journey of negotiation, the role of the human factor unfolds. It's about more than just finding middle ground; it's about guiding the couple to a profound understanding of their own needs. Through this understanding, the path to open communication materializes, paving the way for compromise and, ultimately, reconciliation.

Shift your perspective to the vibrant tapestry of family life. Consider parents who, though deeply committed, harbor distinct parenting styles. Negotiating in personal relationships becomes a linchpin in the harmonious functioning of such families. Here, it's not merely about finding middle ground—it's about honoring each other's unique approaches. The human factor calls for parents to engage in dialogue that transcends compromise, fostering an environment where different parenting styles coexist, contributing to a harmonious family atmosphere.

Further, contemplate the nuanced dynamics of friendships, where the bonds are cherished, but conflicts can surface due to differing expectations. In the realm of negotiating in personal relationships, friends are called to action. Their journey involves candid conversations that embrace vulnerability. It's about acknowledging each other's viewpoints, not just in theory but in practice, to reach solutions that not only preserve their cherished bond but also respect individual preferences.

As you embrace win-win communication in your personal life, remember that it's a journey of mutual growth and understanding. It's about choosing to approach conflicts with empathy and active listening, not as battles to be won but as opportunities to strengthen the connections that matter most to you. By applying these principles in personal relationships, you can become the source of that transformative experience for your loved ones.

EXERCISES

WIN-WIN CHALLENGE

Choose a personal relationship that's been strained. Plan a heartfelt conversation where you express your feelings and actively listen to theirs.

WIN-WIN INSIGHTS

"Love, understanding, and compromise are the foundations of healthy personal relationships. The human factor can mend even the deepest rifts."

Chapter 8 — THE HUMAN FACTOR IN BUSINESS

"In business, I've discovered that my purpose is to do my best to my utmost ability every day. That's my standard. I learned early in my life that I could accomplish anything I wanted to."
    ~ Donald Trump

In the previous chapters, we've explored the principles of win-win communication in more personal contexts. Now, we turn our focus to the world of business, where the human factor plays a pivotal role in achieving success and sustainability. Let's explore the complexities of business negotiations and how embracing the win-win mindset can lead to fruitful outcomes.

In the business world, win-win communication is not just a nice-to-have; it's a necessity. Successful companies understand that fostering a collaborative environment through active listening, empathy, and finding common ground can be the difference between growth and stagnation.

Consider a real-world example from my career: a company acquisition. The purchase of the organization I worked for by another firm required intricate negotiations, particularly concerning employee-owned stocks and job security.

In this case, the win-win approach prevailed, ensuring that employees were not only protected but also benefited financially. The purchasing company also achieved its objectives, resulting in a successful business deal. This exemplifies how win-win communication can lead to mutually beneficial outcomes for all parties involved.

However, the business landscape is not always a win-win paradise. In fiercely competitive industries, companies often face situations where a win-lose agenda becomes the norm. The need for survival can sometimes push businesses to adopt strategies that may not align with the win-win approach. It's a stark reality of the corporate world where market share and profit margins dictate actions. In such cases, it may be necessary to make difficult choices, such as paying premium prices to secure resources or outbidding competitors for new business opportunities.

Peel back the layers of the corporate world, and let's showcase how the human factor, through empathy, trust, and unwavering commitment, is the cornerstone of success in the dynamic world of business. It's not just about deals and profits; it's about people—the heartbeat of any enterprise.

Visualize two corporate giants engaged in a merger, a complex dance of strategies and assets. Amidst the intricate negotiations, what shines through is a commitment to the people—the employees. Here, the human factor steps into the spotlight as leaders, with unwavering resolve, prioritize the well-being of their workforce. Through transparent communication and collaborative planning, they chart a path for a seamless integration, recognizing that success hinges on the people who bring the organizations to life.

Picture a scenario were employees, the lifeblood of the company, harbor concerns about management decisions. The human factor takes center stage, showcasing the art of listening and empathy. With this approach, management emerges not as distant decision-makers but as active listeners, attentively heeding the feedback of their teams. Trust and mutual respect become the cornerstones of a culture that thrives on openness and cooperation.

Transitioning to the retail sector, immerse yourself in the essence of customer-centricity. Here, the human factor in business becomes a beacon, illuminating the path to success. It's not merely about transactions but about relationships. It's about employees who wholeheartedly delve into understanding customer needs, crafting personalized solutions, and forging connections that transcend a single purchase. In this realm, the human factor is the driving force behind lasting customer relationships.

While win-lose scenarios still exist, it doesn't mean that the win-win mindset has no place in business. On the contrary, it's essential to strike a balance and identify opportunities for win-win outcomes whenever possible. By doing so, companies can build lasting relationships with customers, suppliers, and employees, which ultimately contribute to long-term success.

Can businesses encourage and implement win-win communication throughout their operations? The answer is a resounding yes. The key lies in nurturing a corporate culture that values collaboration, understanding, and the well-being of all stakeholders. Employees who embrace the win-win mindset will naturally work towards the company's growth and prosperity.

Active listening and empathy are essential drivers in a business environment. When employees feel heard, valued, and understood, they are more likely to engage with the win-win mindset in their daily work activities. This not only enhances job satisfaction but also contributes to increased productivity and innovation. It's a win-win for both the employees and the organization.

As we've explored throughout, there's an ethical dimension to win-win communication. It aligns with the timeless principle of "do unto others as you would have them do unto you." In the business context, this translates to maintaining transparency, honesty, and integrity in all interactions. By adhering to ethical considerations, businesses can foster trust and credibility, which are crucial elements for long-term success.

Chapter 8 reaffirms the significance of the human factor in the business world. It highlights the tangible benefits of win-win communication for both companies and their employees. By finding common ground, fostering a collaborative spirit, and adhering to ethical principles, businesses can thrive in an ever-changing and competitive environment. This chapter underscores the enduring importance of the win-win approach in the corporate arena.

EXERCISES

WIN-WIN CHALLENGE

At your workplace, identify a situation where a win-win approach could lead to a better outcome for everyone involved. Initiate a discussion and seek consensus.

WIN-WIN INSIGHTS

"The business world thrives when win-win strategies are adopted. It's not just about profit; it's about fostering trust and lasting partnerships."

Chapter 9 — THE ETHICS OF WIN-WIN COMMUNICATION

"In the end, it's not the years in your life that count. It's the life in your years."

~ Abraham Lincoln

In this journey through the art of win-win communication and negotiation, we have explored the nuances of the "human factor." It's been a comprehensive exploration, delving into the relevance of the human factor in various aspects of life and shedding light on the challenges associated with traditional win-lose approaches. We've also discussed the transformative power of empathy, the significance of active listening, and the art of finding common ground. We've ventured into the territory of overcoming obstacles and resistance and applied these principles to personal relationships and the dynamic world of business.

Now, as we this point, it's time to address a fundamental aspect of win-win communication – ethics. This isn't just about making deals; it's about making deals that are ethical, principled, and grounded in the values that define us. Our journey has brought us to this point, where we need to understand the boundaries, principles, and ethical considerations that govern win-win negotiations.

So, what is ethical communication in the context of win-win negotiation? It's about understanding that even in the pursuit of mutually beneficial outcomes, certain principles guide our interactions. These principles are rooted in honesty, respect, and a deep consideration of others' perspectives and needs. The principals form the ethical compass that ensures we navigate negotiations with integrity.

Our exploration has revealed that empathy plays a central role in this ethical landscape. To be truly ethical in our negotiations, we must genuinely understand others' viewpoints, respecting their feelings and needs. Active listening, as we've discussed, enables us to practice this empathy effectively. The act of hearing others, not just listening to their words, promotes understanding and ethical interactions.

In the exercises, we have encountered situations where ethical considerations became paramount in the decision-making process. The dilemma of whether to compromise our ethical values or uphold them is a real challenge in win-win negotiation. We've learned that ethical boundaries are not just theoretical constructs; they are practical guidelines that influence our decisions in profound ways.

In this pursuit of ethical win-win communication, we've come to appreciate the cultural and contextual variations in ethical standards. Our world is diverse, and respecting these differences is integral to ethical negotiations. This calls for the skill of understanding, respecting, and adapting to the cultural and contextual nuances while remaining true to our ethical values.

In the realm of win-win communication, ethics take center stage with transparency, responsibility, and integrity serving as guiding principles. This stands as a testament to the enduring influence of ethical behavior in nurturing trust, fostering harmony, and propelling progress in our interconnected world.

Envision a company navigating the labyrinth of complex data privacy regulations. Here, the ethics of win-win communication manifest in transparency, a cornerstone of trust. The company seeks to emerge as a guardian of individuals' privacy rights, diligently seeking consent for data usage. This ethical stance not only ensures compliance with the law but also fosters a culture of respect and integrity.

Continuing the focus on the corporate arena, where a company's approach to social responsibility is under scrutiny. Here, the ethics of win-win communication materialize as a commitment to ethical business practices, environmental sustainability, and community support. The company becomes a steward of societal well-being, aligning its success with the greater good. In this narrative, business transcends profits, becoming a force for positive change.

Finally, let your imagination navigate to a crisis-ridden landscape where a company grapples with unfavorable media coverage. In this tumultuous scenario, the ethics of win-win communication demand accountability and transparency. The company takes responsibility for its actions, addresses public concerns candidly, and undertakes corrective measures. This ethical resolve becomes the cornerstone of rebuilding trust with the public, demonstrating that even in adversity, ethics remain unwavering.

The final question we face is how to strike the balance between maintaining ethical communication and achieving our goals. In a world often driven by fierce competition, it's easy to lose sight of ethical principles in the pursuit of success. However, our journey has shown us that success is not the endpoint; it's the journey itself.

As we conclude our exploration of the ethics of win-win communication, the lesson is clear: success is not about reaching the destination at any cost; it's about reaching it with our ethical integrity intact. The journey is just as important as the outcome, and in our ethical journey, we embrace the spirit of the "human factor," where empathy, understanding, and ethical principles converge to create a world where everyone can thrive.

EXERCISES

WIN-WIN CHALLENGE

Examine your personal code of ethics. Reflect on a time when adhering to ethical principles led to a win-win situation. Share your story with someone.

WIN-WIN INSIGHTS

"Integrity and ethics are the bedrock of win-win communication. They ensure that everyone feels respected and valued."

Chapter 10 — MASTERING THE HUMAN FACTOR

"The only limit to our realization of tomorrow will be our doubts of today."

~ Franklin D. Roosevelt

We've traversed various landscapes throughout this journey. From understanding the significance of the "human factor" to breaking free from the limitations of win-lose thinking, from the transformative power of empathy to the art of active listening and finding common ground, we've discussed overcoming obstacles and resistance. We've even applied these principles to personal relationships and to the world of business while considering the ethics that underpin our negotiations.

Now, as we approach the final chapter, the question arises: how do we truly master the human factor and integrate it into our lives? How do we ensure that this isn't just a set of techniques but a way of living, a philosophy that shapes our interactions and decisions?

The answer lies in reflection and practice. Mastering the human factor begins with a commitment to self-awareness and continuous improvement. We've learned that empathy is at the heart of win-win communication, but it's not something you switch on and off. It's a part of you, a lens through which you view the world and engage with others.

This journey hasn't just been about acquiring skills; it's been about embracing a mindset, a way of being. To master the human factor, it's essential to continually practice and refine the art of empathy. It's about consistently striving to understand others, putting yourself in their shoes, and considering their feelings and needs.

We've also seen the value of active listening in our communication. It's not merely a technique but a way of approaching conversations. To master the human factor, you must make active listening a part of your daily life. It's about giving your full attention, hearing not just words but the emotions and perspectives behind them. It's about fostering a culture of genuine understanding.

Our exploration has shown that finding common ground is the foundation of win-win communication. To master the human factor, you must make this your guiding principle. Seek solutions that will benefit all parties. Whether it's in your personal life or business endeavors, the win-win mindset should be your compass.

Overcoming obstacles and resistance isn't just a matter of strategy; it's a test of patience and determination. To master the human factor, remember that perseverance and empathy are your allies. In the face of opposition, keep your goals and the well-being of all parties in sight.

In these examples we show how the profound impact of mastering the human factor in leadership, where it fosters unity, ignites positive change, and ushers in a brighter future in various leadership scenarios, mastering the human factor emerges as a transformative force. Picture an educational institution where a dedicated principal aspires to cultivate a positive learning environment. Here, mastery involves inspiring teachers, students, and parents, instilling a sense of belonging, and nurturing a collaborative educational community.

Within the realm of nonprofit organizations, envision a passionate leader dedicated to a noble cause. True mastery of the human factor resides in the leader's ability to empower volunteers and staff, communicate a compelling vision, and harness collective efforts to effectively realize the organization's mission, by listening to others ideas, thoughts, and viewpoints.

Lastly, consider a community leader deeply engaged in addressing local issues. In this context, mastering the human factor entails building meaningful connections with community members, embracing diverse perspectives, and collaboratively forging solutions that enhance the overall quality of life for residents.

As we've explored, win-win communication isn't confined to the boardroom; it extends to personal relationships. Mastering the human factor in personal life means practicing empathy, understanding, and compromise. It's about building stronger, more meaningful connections with loved ones, even in the face of disagreements.

In the business world, embracing the human factor is a choice that leads to success. As you pursue your professional goals, remember that prioritizing mutually beneficial outcomes can transform the way you conduct business. It's about fostering an environment where everyone thrives.

Our journey has also emphasized the ethical considerations of win-win communication. To master the human factor, you must recognize that integrity and respect should always guide your actions. Even in the midst of competition, ethical principles are non-negotiable.

Now, as we wrap this up and conclude our exploration of the human factor, the call to action is clear: practice, embody, and champion the principles of win-win communication in every facet of your life. Mastering the human factor isn't about perfection; it's about progress. It's about becoming an advocate for a more empathetic, understanding, and ethical world. It's about sharing the lessons you've learned and inspiring others to join you on this transformative journey.

Let us remember that the human factor isn't just a concept; it's the essence of human connection and the key to unlocking success through collaborative negotiation. Embrace it, live it, and watch the world transform.

EXERCISES

WIN-WIN CHALLENGE

Commit to applying the principles of win-win communication to at least one significant aspect of your life. Record your progress and challenges in a journal.

WIN-WIN INSIGHTS

"Mastering the human factor is a lifelong journey. As you embrace it, you'll discover that every day offers opportunities for growth and connection."

Chapter 11 — Practical Tips for Mastering Win-Win Communication

In our journey through the world of win-win communication and negotiation, you've gained insights and learned essential principles. Now, it's time to equip you with practical tips that will help you apply these concepts in your daily life.

Remember, the true power of win-win communication lies in its application.

Active Listening for Everyday life

It's not just in professional meetings where active listening works wonders. Apply it at home during family discussions, with friends during catchups, and whenever you engage in conversations. Try to be fully present and attentive.

Empathy beyond boundaries

Extend your empathy beyond personal relationships. Practice it when dealing with colleagues, clients, or even strangers. This simple act can defuse tense situations and create better connections with everyone you encounter.

The art of compromise

Recognize that compromise isn't a sign of weakness but a pillar of strength. Be willing to find middle ground in various aspects of life, from deciding what to have for dinner to resolving disputes at work.

Questioning techniques

Use open-ended questions to encourage deeper conversations. When you ask, "How do you see this situation?" instead of "Do you agree?" you invite more meaningful responses.

Communicate clearly and concisely

Remember that effective communication is not just about speaking but also about being understood. Avoid jargon or complex language when a simpler explanation will do.

The power of silence

Don't underestimate the value of pauses in a conversation. Give the other person time to process their thoughts and respond. This can lead to more thoughtful and authentic interactions.

Negotiation at home

Apply negotiation tactics within your personal life. Whether it's determining household chores, planning vacations, or discussing finances, the principles of finding common ground and aiming for mutual benefits are just as relevant.

Managing workplace conflict

In a professional setting, use win-win techniques to manage and resolve conflicts. These approaches can lead to more productive and harmonious work environments.

Keeping a win-win journal

Consider keeping a journal where you document your win-win communication experiences. Write down situations where you applied these principles and the outcomes achieved. This not only reinforces your learning but also serves as a reference for future interactions.

The ripple effect

Be aware of the positive ripple effect your win-win communication can have on others. By modeling these behaviors, you inspire those around you to adopt similar approaches, fostering a culture of collaboration and understanding.

Lifelong learning

Embrace the idea that mastering win-win communication is an ongoing journey. Continue to learn, adapt, and grow, seeking out additional resources or courses that can expand your knowledge and skills.

Remember, the essence of win-win communication is not just about securing favorable outcomes for yourself but also about creating a world where everyone can thrive. It's a journey that starts with understanding, empathy, and active listening, and it's a journey worth embarking on.

As you integrate these practical tips into your life, you'll find that win-win communication becomes a way of living, a mindset, and a bridge to greater understanding and fulfillment in all your interactions. You have the tools and knowledge; now it's your turn to make them work for you.

Chapter 12— Win-Win Communication in Action - Case Studies

Throughout this book, we've delved into the art of win-win communication and negotiation, exploring its principles, applications, and the profound impact it can have on various aspects of life. In this chapter, we'll bring these concepts to life through real-world case studies that showcase how individuals and organizations have harnessed the power of win-win communication to achieve remarkable outcomes.

As you read through these stories, consider how you can apply the lessons learned to your own life and endeavors. These case studies are a testament to the transformative power of win-win communication and serve as a source of inspiration for your journey toward mastering this art.

CASE STUDY 1: BRIDGING THE GENERATION GAP IN THE WORKPLACE

In this case, we'll look at a multinational corporation that faced challenges in integrating a multigenerational workforce. Through win-win strategies, they not only resolved generational conflicts but also enhanced productivity and innovation.

The Challenge:

A multinational corporation with a diverse workforce spanning several generations, from Baby Boomers to Generation Z, faced challenges in creating a harmonious work environment. Generation gaps led to miscommunication, misunderstandings, and a decline in collaboration and innovation.

The Win-Win Solution:

To address this challenge, the organization introduced cross-generational mentoring programs, where younger employees could learn from the wisdom of their older counterparts. Additionally, they established intergenerational focus groups to foster open dialogue, encouraging employees to share their experiences, challenges, and ideas. The organization recognized that each generation had unique strengths and insights to offer.

The Outcome:

By embracing a win-win mindset, the corporation witnessed a significant transformation. Teams started working more effectively, benefiting from the diverse perspectives and skills of all generations. The company's innovation and creativity skyrocketed as employees learned to collaborate and leverage each other's strengths. Furthermore, employee satisfaction and retention rates improved, and the company's reputation as an inclusive workplace flourished.

CASE STUDY 2: A FAMILY REUNITED THROUGH COMMUNICATION

This heartwarming story recounts the journey of a family torn apart by misunderstandings and conflict. We'll uncover how win-win communication played a pivotal role in bringing them back together, rebuilding trust, and strengthening family bonds.

The Challenge:

A family was torn apart by unresolved conflicts and misunderstandings, leaving strained relationships and emotional scars. Members stopped communicating and distanced themselves from each other.

The Win-Win Solution:

With the intervention of a family therapist who understood win-win communication, the family embarked on a journey to healing. Each family member was encouraged to share their feelings, perspectives, and expectations openly. The therapist facilitated empathetic listening and guided the family in finding common ground, emphasizing their shared history and love for each other.

The Outcome:

Through persistent efforts, the family members began to reconnect on a deeper level. They mended their relationships and learned to appreciate each other's differences. The win-win approach led to stronger bonds, trust, and a newfound sense of unity. It not only reunited the family but also empowered them to handle future conflicts in a healthier way.

CASE STUDY 3: A WIN-WIN APPROACH TO ENTREPRENEURIAL SUCCESS

In this case study, we'll follow the entrepreneurial journey of a start-up founder who leveraged win-win communication to secure critical partnerships, navigate industry challenges, and ultimately scale the business to new heights.

The Challenge:

A tech start-up faced hurdles in establishing partnerships and securing its place in a competitive market. Traditional win-lose negotiations often left them at a disadvantage.

The Win-Win Solution:

The start-up shifted its approach to negotiations by emphasizing value creation for all parties involved. They sought mutually beneficial agreements with partners and investors, focusing on building relationships that went beyond immediate transactions.

The Outcome:

This win-win strategy allowed the start-up to form strategic alliances with key industry players. Over time, the collaborative approach resulted in the development of innovative products and services that met market demands. The company not only survived but thrived in a competitive landscape, proving that a win-win approach can lead to entrepreneurial success.

CASE STUDY 4: NEGOTIATING FOR A SUSTAINABLE FUTURE

We'll explore the journey of an environmental activist who used win-win communication to drive change and influence government policies. This case demonstrates how win-win strategies can be a powerful force for creating a more sustainable world.

The Challenge:

A manufacturing company faced recurring disputes and strained relations between its workforce and the management team. These conflicts hindered productivity and led to high employee turnover.

The Win-Win Solution:

The company's HR department introduced a comprehensive employee engagement program that fostered open channels of communication. They organized regular town hall meetings where employees could voice their concerns and share their ideas. Management actively listened, demonstrated empathy, and worked on implementing solutions that addressed the employees' grievances.

The Outcome:

As a result of implementing the win-win approach, employee morale and job satisfaction improved significantly. The company experienced a drop in employee turnover and an increase in overall productivity. Both management and employees began to see themselves as part of a united team, working collaboratively to achieve common goals.

CASE STUDY 5: THE TRANSFORMATION OF A STRUGGLING NONPROFIT

In this inspiring example, we'll dive into the story of a struggling nonprofit organization on the brink of closure. Through the application of win-win communication principles, they not only saved the organization but also expanded their impact and outreach.

The Challenge:

An environmentally conscious non-profit organization sought to promote sustainable practices in a community resistant to change. The community was resistant to any initiative they perceived as an imposition on their way of life.

The Win-Win Solution:

The organization adopted a win-win approach by actively listening to the community's concerns and understanding their values. They tailored their sustainability programs to align with local cultural practices, emphasizing how these changes could benefit both the environment and the community.

The Outcome:

By taking this approach, the non-profit organization successfully influenced the community to embrace sustainable practices. Local residents began to see the benefits of a cleaner environment, cost savings, and a stronger sense of community. The win-win strategy allowed the organization to achieve its environmental goals while respecting the community's way of life.

Conclusion— EMBRACING THE ESSENCE OF THE HUMAN FACTOR

To conclude this journey through the profound art of win-win communication, it's time to bask in the wisdom we've amassed and recognize the monumental impact it can have on our lives. The concept of the "human factor" is not merely an abstract idea but a living, breathing philosophy that permeates every facet of our existence. It's the guiding light in the labyrinth of communication and the elixir that fuels harmonious relationships.

Reflecting upon my grandma's sagacious counsel, I am reminded of the invaluable life lessons she bestowed upon us. "To connect with others," she once told me, "You must first connect with yourself." It's through understanding and embracing our own humanity that we gain the capacity to resonate with the humanity in others. Empathy, the cornerstone of win-win communication, allows us to forge connections and transcend differences.

In the intricate tapestry of win-win negotiation, active listening is the thread that stitches it all together. My grandma would often impart, "In the silence, you hear the echoes of their soul." Through active listening, we amplify our understanding of others and truly grasp their needs, aspirations, and emotions. It's in these moments of genuine connection that win-win solutions emerge.

In the realm of personal anecdotes and shared experiences, we've witnessed the human factor in action. From the memorable lessons learned in the intricate dance of personal relationships to the art of resolving conflicts, the human factor has consistently proven to be the compass guiding us through the storms of life.

Drawing from our stories and experiences, we've observed that the human factor is not a technique but a way of being. It's in the world of business where success stories have illuminated the path. By prioritizing win-win strategies, companies have not only achieved profitability but have also left legacies of goodwill. They have demonstrated my grandma's words: "In every interaction, leave a piece of your kindness."

So, what's our call to action as we conclude this enlightening journey? My grandma's wisdom provides the answer: "As you learn, teach. As you achieve, inspire."

Let us empower ourselves and, in turn, empower those around us to embrace the human factor. To understand, to listen, to find common ground, to overcome obstacles, and to uphold ethical values. Let us be torchbearers of empathy and champions of win-win communication in every corner of our lives.

The stories we've shared, the experiences we've gathered, and the knowledge we've unlocked are not meant to be confined to the pages of this book. They are meant to be woven into the tapestry of our daily existence, guiding our interactions, shaping our decisions, and redefining our relationships.

The human factor is a way of life, and it's a path to a brighter, more compassionate world. As we bid farewell to this book, let us embrace the essence of the human factor wholeheartedly, for within it lies the key to unlocking the doors of success, happiness, and meaningful connections.

The journey is yours to continue, and the world is waiting for your imprint. In the words of my grandma, "Go forth and create a world where win-win communication thrives, where understanding reigns, and where the human factor shines brightly."

Here are 10 key takeaways that you can practice each day:

Empathy: Take a moment to understand others' perspectives before reacting. Practice empathy in your interactions, both personal and professional.

Active Listening: Focus on truly listening to what others are saying without interrupting or formulating your response. Validate their feelings and concerns through attentive listening.

Win-Win Mindset: Embrace the idea that cooperation and collaboration lead to better outcomes than competition. Look for solutions that benefit all parties involved.

Finding Common Ground: Seek areas of agreement and shared goals in your relationships and negotiations. Building common ground fosters understanding and paves the way for productive discussions.

Effective Communication: Strive for clarity and transparency in your communication. Express yourself honestly and respectfully and encourage others to do the same.

Resolving Conflict Constructively: Approach conflicts with an open mind and a willingness to find mutually beneficial solutions. Focus on problem-solving rather than assigning blame.

Prioritizing Relationships: Value the people in your life and invest time and effort into nurturing meaningful connections. Strong relationships form the foundation of a fulfilling life.

Ethical Conduct: Always act with integrity and honesty, even when faced with difficult decisions. Upholding ethical principles builds trust and credibility in your personal and professional life.

Leadership through Service: Lead by example and serve others with humility and compassion. Leadership is about empowering others and creating opportunities for their growth and success.

Continuous Learning and Growth: Commit to lifelong learning and personal development. Stay curious, explore new perspectives, and embrace opportunities for growth in all areas of your life.

By incorporating these principles into your daily life, you can cultivate stronger relationships, make more informed decisions, and create a positive impact in your community and beyond.

Thank you for embarking on this enlightening journey, and may the human factor guide your path to greater understanding, fulfillment, and success.

May your path be filled with empathy, active listening, and win-win solutions, for it's through these principles that you'll not only communicate effectively but also change the world, one conversation at a time.

About the Author

David Lask is a seasoned professional with over two decades of experience in information security, IT management, and business operations. His journey has been marked by a commitment to excellence, innovation, and ethical leadership. Throughout his career, David has been at the forefront of developing and implementing security policies and procedures to ensure compliance with state regulations while safeguarding sensitive data. His expertise in risk management, privacy compliance, and incident response has been instrumental in driving organizational success and fostering a culture of collaboration and innovation.

David's passion for sharing knowledge and expertise extends beyond his professional endeavors. As a certified instructor in private postsecondary and vocational education, he is dedicated to empowering others with the skills and insights they need to succeed. In his book, "The Human Factor: Mastering the Art of Win-Win Communication," David offers invaluable insights and practical strategies for navigating the complexities of modern communication. Through a focus on building strong relationships, navigating negotiations, and unlocking potential, David inspires readers to thrive personally and professionally in today's interconnected world.